ISBN: 978-1-7355223-2-6

THE RECOVERY ROOM

A Self-Love Journey for the Broken, the Healing, and the Hopeful

By Eric T. Roscoe

"The Lord is close to the brokenhearted and saves those who are crushed in spirit." — Psalm 34:18

"He heals the brokenhearted and binds up their wounds." — Psalm 147:3

"The Lord is my shepherd; I shall not want… He restores my soul." — Psalm 23:1,3

Dedication

To every soul who's ever tried to love from a broken place… May this journey lead you to healing, wholeness, and the kind of love that begins with you.

Acknowledgments

First and foremost, I give all glory, honor, and praise to God the Father, the Son, and the Holy Spirit — the source of my healing, wisdom, and strength. Without Your love and guidance, this book would not exist. You walked with me through every valley, spoke to me in every quiet place, and restored what I thought was lost. Thank You for being my

Shepherd, my Counselor, my Deliverer, and my Friend.

This book is not just a work of reflection — it is a testimony of Your grace, Your patience, and Your power to restore the brokenhearted. May every word bring You glory and draw the reader closer to Your heart.

To my Kingdom family and support system, especially my Salt Hub family —thank you for standing with me through every season of this journey. Your encouragement, intercession, accountability, and presence have meant more than words can express. I'm forever grateful.

To my daughters — Keely, Kylah, and Kalli — thank you for inspiring me to become better, not just for myself, but for you. Your love is my motivation, and your future is worth every sacrifice. This book is for you.

Foreword

There comes a point in every person's life when survival is no longer enough. We begin to crave something deeper something more than simply "getting by" after life has shaken us to the core. We long to be healed, made whole, and fully awakened to the life God intended for us.

That's where The Recovery Room meets you. Not in perfection. Not after the storm has passed. But right in the middle of the process, when you are still finding your way back to yourself.

Eric Roscoe has penned a work that is more than words on a page. It is a prophetic invitation to step into a sacred space where honesty meets healing, where pain collides with promise, and where your broken places are not hidden they are redeemed. This book is a spiritual blueprint and a practical roadmap for those who refuse to let their trauma be their tomb.

I believe this book carries a prophetic sound a call for men and women to return to the place of recovery not as victims, but as over-comers. Eric doesn't offer quick fixes or hollow inspiration. Instead, he lays out natural roadways to personal restoration, anchored in spiritual truth, emotional honesty, and intentional growth.

What makes this message powerful is that it's written from the heart of someone who has walked through it. These are not theories. These are testimonies, battle scars, and victories. The Recovery Room doesn't just talk about healing it creates space for it to happen.

As I turned these pages, I could feel the Father's voice echoing: "This is the season where I restore what was broken, and make whole what was fractured." The beauty of recovery is not in pretending the pain never happened, but in discovering that God was always working behind the scenes to rewrite your story.

My prayer is that as you read this book, you don't simply admire the words, but that you encounter the Healer Himself. May each chapter be a doorway leading you back to your identity, your value, and your God-given purpose.

If you allow it, this book will help you:
- Face the truth without shame.
- Walk through healing without fear.
- And embrace your future without apology.

Eric Roscoe has offered us a kingdom tool a manual for those who are ready to recover, rebuild, and rise again.

May The Recovery Room be more than a book to you; may it become a turning point.

Welcome to your recovery.
Welcome to the room where your story is not finished.
Welcome to the beginning of your new chapter.

With love and gratitude,

William Cornigans

Table of Contents

Chapter 1 — Self-Discovery

"The Lord is close to the brokenhearted and saves those who are crushed in spirit."
— Psalm 34:18

The Universal Experience of Pain

One of the things we all have in common is that we are subject to human experiences including strengths, weaknesses, and failures. Whether in the corporate world, the church, or any kind of relationship, no one is exempt.

Hurt, pain, rejection, betrayal, heartbreak, offense, disappointment, and abandonment are part of the human journey. We either have experienced them or will at some point. This means we will all, at some time, need to learn how to navigate and process the unpleasant feelings and emotions connected to those experiences.

The Power of Letting Go

Regardless of what happened or who did what, the best advice I can give you is simple but not always easy: let it go. For some, that may be easier said than done. But choosing to forgive the one who wronged you is the first step toward reclaiming your power. One simple decision to forgive can set you free in many ways.

When you understand that forgiveness is for you and not the person who harmed you, you can release them from their debt, just as Jesus released you from yours. You can also take responsibility for your part and how you choose to move forward. Forgiveness doesn't mean you must continue in relationship with them it means giving the burden they caused you back to God.

"Cast all your cares, [all your anxieties, worries, and all your concerns once and for all]on Him because He cares for you." — 1 Peter
5:7 AMP
"Forgive others, and your Father in heaven will forgive you." — Mark 11:25 KJ

God has created a binding contract that works through the law of love.

Accountability Over Excuses

"No one is perfect, right?" This is something we often say when we do something wrong or try to justify our actions.

Although there's some truth in that, it doesn't help us grow. We don't have to use our imperfections as an excuse to avoid accountability. Instead, we can choose to strengthen the weaker areas that cause us to fall short. We should always strive to be better for God first, then for ourselves, and for those around us. The truth is, we are often just as guilty as we are victims in our failures and mistakes. Yet, we typically want to place the blame solely on others.

The reality is this: it takes two for a situation to go wrong or right. Relational skills, self-awareness, and understanding are essential in improving the quality of every relationship — whether business, marriage, parent-child, or friendship.

Two Types of People

Over time, I've discovered there are generally two kinds of people we encounter in life:

1. Those who make mistakes, but can admit, acknowledge, apologize, and learn from them.
2. Those who struggle to admit when they're wrong, avoid accountability, and find it hard to

apologize — making it difficult for them to grow or love others effectively.

This second type often casts themselves as the victim and rarely apologizes, even when they may be the cause of the problem. Depending on where you are in your healing journey, it may be necessary to create boundaries with people like this.

Lessons From a Past Relationship

In one of my past relationships, I faced this behavior directly. Some would call it narcissistic — everything revolved around them. They lifted themselves up while tearing others down and could be selfish and manipulative.

But relationships are meant to be a two-way street. To flourish, both people must learn to interact better. That requires love, intentionality, maturity, understanding, and mutual respect.

Let's be honest mastering this takes a lifetime. Unless someone is willing to take responsibility for their contribution to a relationship, good or bad, it won't work. Accountability is the foundation.

Being accountable is a sign of three powerful traits:
- Self-awareness
- Mental and emotional intelligence
- Maturity and responsibility

Leading Yourself First

These three traits point to something crucial: you must first be able to lead yourself before you can lead anyone else.

Most women would agree they prefer a man who can lead in love, protect in love, and provide (mentally, emotionally, and financially) in love. Yet, many have difficulty recognizing this when it shows up because it feels foreign compared to their past experiences.

I've been there. I've experienced rejection from someone I genuinely wanted to get to know. But I chose not to let rejection make me bitter. Instead, I learned to appreciate rejection because it revealed my value. I refuse to settle for someone who doesn't recognize my worth or appreciate me as a person. Worth isn't just financial — it's holistic.

When Love Isn't Love

I was married for nearly seven years. My ex-wife wouldn't leave because of the financial security I provided, but she consistently disrespected me and verbally and mentally abused me. As I grew in my understanding of God's love, I realized that what I was experiencing wasn't love. That's not how you treat someone you say you love. Because we were both broken, I chose to leave. As long as I provided everything, she wasn't going anywhere. Looking back, I don't regret walking away — that's where my healing began.

"Hurting people hurt people." We both exchanged words that cut deep. Rejection taught me valuable lessons: unless a person matches your effort and energy, they're not the right one for you. Rejection isn't always bad when you understand your worth.

Learning to Respond With Grace

Another mark of maturity is learning how to respond under pressure — to circumstances, disappointments, and life's unexpected turns.
Everyone has shortcomings, but not everyone admits them or works on them when their partner addresses them. Usually, one of two things happens:

1. The couple chooses honesty and works through the issue together.

2. One person becomes
defensive, offended, or shut down —
putting up walls that make matters
worse.

This defensive behavior often stems
from pride, a pride that prioritizes
self over understanding. Humility,
however, listens even when what's
said isn't entirely accurate because it
values the other person's feelings.
This makes all the difference in
building healthy, lasting
relationships.

Healthy People Build Healthy Relationships

For a relationship to be healthy, both individuals must be healthy. Otherwise, toxic behaviors will surface from unaddressed wounds.

Great marriages and strong relationships require work from both sides. It's not easy, but anything worth keeping is worth fighting for. I see marriage and relationships as an investment — requiring:

- Communication
- Consideration
- Compromise
- Willingness
- Loyalty
- Understanding
- Mutual submission

When both partners contribute to these, the best results follow.

My Journey of Healing

Since my divorce in December 2017, I've been on a self-love journey. Everything you're about to read in this book flows from what I've learned along the way.

If you desire to grow as an individual, strengthen your marriage or relationships, or heal from past pain, this book is for you. If you're single and have experienced disappointment in dating or marriage, this can help you too.

And most importantly, if you desire to deepen your relationship with God and heal from childhood trauma, invite Him into your journey. Make Him the center of your relationships and begin your personal self-love journey. I didn't know this before my divorce but God led me straight into that healing process.

Recovery Takeaway:
True healing begins with self-awareness, forgiveness, and God at the center. Your past may have

shaped you, but it does not have to define you.

Recovery Declaration:
"I declare that my heart is no longer a slave to emotions, disappointments, or past wounds." I rise in divine strength, leading my heart under the Lord's guidance. Every misplaced affection is being realigned in Jesus name!"

"My expectations are no longer chained to man but anchored in God. From this day forward, my heart will

follow divine direction and not
temporary emotions. I decree healing,
order, and divine timing
over every matter of my heart."

Chapter 1 - Self-Discovery

Reflection & Journaling

Reflection Moment:

What parts of your identity have been shaped by pain or rejection?

Journal Prompt:

Where do you feel God calling you to rediscover your true self?

_____

_____

_____

_____

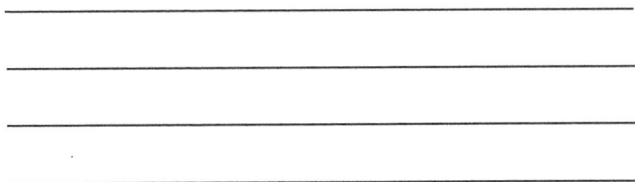

Chapter 2 — When Love Misplaces you

"Let every person be quick to hear, slow to speak, slow to anger."
— James 1:19

Building Bridges, Not Barriers

Consider this: two individuals, each with different backgrounds, experiences, and perspectives, are coming together for a shared purpose to learn how to become one and work together.

True communication is more than just exchanging words. It's about connection. It requires patience, humility, flexibility, and most importantly, a willingness to compromise. By compromise, I mean learning to pick your battles, being open to honest dialogue, and choosing to prefer one another in ways that express love not just in the way you want to love, but in the way your partner needs to be loved.

This means learning your partner's love language and communicating in their language, not just your own. Being understanding involves allowing each other to be vulnerable, open to growth, and willing to make the changes necessary for both of you to become better individually and together.

Being understanding doesn't mean agreeing with everything. It means learning your partner's triggers, strengths, and weaknesses, hearing their heart, and choosing empathy over defensiveness or gaslighting. Throughout this journey, I've been learning the power of improving my personal listening skills because listening is one of the most powerful love languages there is.

The Power of Listening

As a couple, it's essential to invest in your listening skills so you can communicate more effectively and minimize misunderstandings. I want to share with you four types of listening that can radically change how you engage in your relationship:

- Appreciative Listening
- Empathic Listening
- Comprehensive Listening
- Critical Listening

You may already be stronger in one area than another, and that's okay. The key is awareness so that you can practice and grow in the areas where you're weaker.

Let's break them down clearly:

1. Appreciative Listening

Appreciative listening is about listening for enjoyment and connection.

Imagine working all day, receiving some really good news, and coming home eager to share it with your significant other. When they lean in, listen with excitement, and genuinely enjoy hearing about your day that's appreciative listening. This kind of listening communicates: "I care about your joy."
It creates a sense of intimacy and allows you to connect mentally and emotionally.

2. Empathic Listening

Empathic listening requires you to show mutual concern and compassion for one another. It means putting yourself in your partner's shoes to understand what they're saying and how they're feeling. This isn't just hearing words; it's about listening with your heart.

When we respond with empathy, we create a safe space where our partner feels seen, heard, and valued.

"People don't care how much you know until they know how much you care."

3. Comprehensive Listening

Comprehensive listening involves active listening with intention. It's the difference between hearing and truly listening. Hearing doesn't require effort. Listening does. Comprehensive listening demands focus, presence, and a desire to understand what's being communicated not just the words, but the meaning behind them.

Mastering this skill will make you a stronger communicator and a more attentive partner. It builds trust because your partner can feel that they have your undivided attention.

4. Critical Listening

Critical listening is slightly different but just as important. This is when you evaluate the content of what's being communicated not to argue or attack, but to process with discernment. It involves critical thinking, sound judgment, and reflection on what you've heard. This type of listening can help resolve conflicts more effectively, because it moves beyond emotion and into understanding, clarity, and wise decision-making.

Listening as a Love Language Learning to integrate these four types of listening appreciative, empathic, comprehensive, and critical can completely change the dynamic of any relationship.

When we listen with love, humility, and intentionality, we not only hear our partner's words we hear their heart. That is where connection deepens, trust is built, and love flourishes.

Recovery Takeaway:
True communication isn't just about talking it's about listening with love. When two people commit to hearing and understanding each other, they

create a foundation that can carry them through any storm.

Recovery Declaration:
"I declare that every place where love misaligned me, God is repositioning me. No longer will my identity be defined by rejection, abandonment, or disappointment. I am being restored to the seat of honor in the presence of my enemies. "My worth is sealed in the One who called me. This is the season where love is no longer a wound but a testimony."

Chapter 2 – When love misplaces you

Reflection Moment:

How have unhealthy communication patterns impacted your healing process? Think about your moments of silence, avoidance, or defensiveness created distance instead of understanding. How did those patterns shape the way you express yourself today—or the way you receive love?

Journal Prompt: What does healthy, honest communication look like for you?

Describe what it feels like when you're heard, seen, and understood. How can you begin to create that kind of communication in your current or future relationships—with others and with yourself?

_____

_____

_____

Chapter 3 — Time of Transparency

"And you will know the truth, and
the truth will set you free."
— John 8:32

My Story:
My previous relationship lasted six
years and ten months, and during
that time I experienced my share of
challenges, victories, and failures.
I've chosen to embrace all three,
because they have shaped me into
the stronger man I am today.

I failed miserably in that relationship for many reasons. I didn't know then what I know now. You could call it on-the-job training. We spent most of our marriage learning each other while also learning how to co-parent our four children.

Take my advice: children are never a reason to get married. While that desire may be honorable and noble, if the two of you are not compatible, the marriage will not work. My ex-wife and I never dated before we got married. I had given my life to Christ

and wanted to "do the right thing."
One thing led to another, and we
found ourselves in a covenant we
weren't fully prepared for.

Those years were incredibly
difficult, but in that difficulty, I
grew. I learned how to become better
for her and for myself. Honestly, it
was my relationship with God that
carried me through. Without Him, I
probably would have walked away
much sooner. But He used that
season to refine, mold, humble, and
reshape me.

I held onto faith, even when it was hard. And because of that, I grew not only spiritually but also in my role as a husband, father, and head of the home.

When Growth Isn't Enough

The hard truth was this: no matter how much I grew, it was never enough for her. No matter how hard I tried, she could not be pleased. It was almost impossible.

Eventually, I had to face the reality that some of the things she needed, I could not give. There were deep soul wounds and childhood traumas that hindered her ability to receive and perceive love. Only God could bring healing in those areas, likely with the help of therapy and counseling but she would have to be open to receive it.

Because she wasn't, that pain began seeping out in other areas of our relationship. And the truth is, she wasn't the only one with wounds.

She had hers, and I had mine.

One of the hardest realizations was recognizing how broken I was and how that brokenness shaped my sense of self-worth. As a child, I was called names, told I wasn't good enough, and those words took root in me. Getting married didn't change that.

This is difficult to admit, but I was a victim of domestic abuse, verbal abuse, and mental abuse. The worst part? My children were exposed to that toxicity. Thank God they were so young they don't remember it but I do.

A Prayer That Changed Everything

One day, after yet another painful disagreement, I sat in confusion and heartbreak. Deep down, I knew what was living in wasn't love it was dysfunction.
In that broken moment, I prayed a prayer I'll never forget:

"Lord, is this going to work five or ten years from now?
If not, allow me to walk away now so I can prepare myself for whoever You have for me."
Shortly after, I received my answer. I knew I had permission to file for divorce.

This was one of the hardest seasons of my life. I had built a deep emotional attachment and soul tie with this woman over nearly seven years. Walking away wasn't easy. But I made the decision to lead my heart instead of being led by my emotions, because I knew this was the right step for me.

Another reason I held on so long was because I knew she would make it difficult for me to have a relationship with our children. She wanted to hurt me not realizing it would hurt them too.

The Power of Being Honest With Yourself

For this reason, I believe that a time of transparency is necessary for anyone who truly desires healing and growth. I want to share some of the wisdom I've gained and begun to apply in my own life.

This is a time to be honest about where we are, what we've done, and what we've allowed. If we walk through life believing that everyone else has hurt us while refusing to acknowledge our own role, we have already missed it.

We cannot always cast ourselves as the victim, no matter what has happened to us. That pain is real. But it does not have to define us.

Maybe this chapter and this book can help redefine you.

This is not about minimizing or dismissing the injustice or pain you've experienced. It's about helping you take responsibility for your own personal growth and decisions, so you can step into a healthier, stronger version of yourself.

Recovery Takeaway:
Transparency isn't weakness it's freedom. Healing begins the moment you stop hiding from the truth of your story and allow God to redefine it.

Recovery Declaration:
"I declare that this is my healing room. Every invisible bruise is being touched by the hand of God. I will no longer mask my pain but yield it to

the One who heals completely. I decree emotional and spiritual wholeness. Where trauma once dictated my decisions, peace shall now govern my path. I am not my pain I am God's restoration in motion.

Chapter 3 – Time of Transparency

Reflection & Journaling

Reflection Moment:

What have you been afraid to admit to yourself or others?

Journal Prompt:

Where can more transparency bring freedom in your life?

_____

_____

_____

_____

_____

_____

Chapter 4 — The Recovery Room

"He heals the brokenhearted and binds up
their wounds."
— Psalm 147:3

Surrendering to the Healer

One of the greatest decisions any of
us can make is to give our hearts to
Christ.
When we accept Jesus as Lord and
Savior and receive the baptism of the
Holy Spirit, we align our spirit,
mind, will, and emotions with the
will of God. And through that

decision, we begin to receive healing and wholeness on our journey to recovery.

We can live without God and build relationships without Him — but it becomes very difficult to maintain them without His covering. It was never God's intention for us to enter marriage or covenant relationships without His leading and blessing.

If we're honest, many of us can admit that we haven't always made the best decisions when it comes to dating or allowing people into our lives. But by His grace, we're still here willing to love again.

Our Response Matters

What if I told you that no matter what evil or wrong people have done to you, at the end of the day, you are not responsible for their actions only for your response and how you choose to move forward?

The Bible urges us to exercise self-control, because the absence of it

leads to instability and poor decision-making. "A person without self-control is like a city with broken-down walls." (Proverbs 25:28)
(NLT)

Without self-control, we become reactive, impulsive, and emotionally volatile. But when God is at the center of our being, influencing our thinking and our choices, He saves us from ourselves.

There are countless times He has kept me from making the wrong move out of impulse and I'm grateful. And even in the times I did make the wrong move, His mercy and kindness covered me.

Facing the Mirror of Healing

The Recovery Room is not a comfortable place. It's not glamorous. It's a real place where you are confronted with the truth about yourself.

Maybe you thought you were healed. Maybe you believed you were ready to date again but then something triggered you, revealing a wound you didn't know was still there.

Don't be alarmed by this. It's actually a sign that God is still working in those hidden areas. With the right people around you supportive friends, mentors, therapists, and a solid faith foundation you'll make it through.

Self-control and emotional
intelligence are skills that can and
must be developed. When
unresolved issues surface, they
reveal areas of arrested development
and unaddressed childhood trauma.
These wounds affect how we
respond, communicate, and love.

Emotional intelligence involves:

- Understanding your own
  emotions
- Regulating your reactions
- Empathizing with others

- Overcoming challenges • Resolving conflict in healthy ways

The Danger of Needing Someone to Complete You

Too often, people look for someone to complete them, to fill a void that only God can fill. But until you address what's inside you first, you'll keep inviting the wrong people into your story. If you've never received Christ, that's your first step. The second is discovering who you are and what He has done for you. Without these foundations, we are not equipped to lead anyone because we cannot yet lead ourselves.

When you begin the journey the right way, you learn your identity and your value.

• Identity reveals who you are and what you were created to do.
• Value teaches you not to settle for less than what God intends for you.

Love and Purpose

Love is a beautiful thing, especially
when you find someone who
genuinely loves and complements
you in every way. But love becomes
dangerous when it distracts you from
your purpose.

We live in a culture that chases love
without understanding their God
given purpose. But it was never
God's will for us to pursue love
above Him.

Pursue God. He reveals your purpose.
Pursue purpose. Love will find you in His timing.

The person God sends will add value, not take it away. If someone enters your life only to extract, they were not sent by God. This is why you must have a clear view of your identity and worth. Without it, you'll settle for less than God's best.

Self-Discovery

For Women

Before you can be found, be intentional about your healing process.

The last thing a good man needs is to carry the weight of other men's mistakes. Give yourself time and space to heal so you can rediscover your worth and value. Emotional instability is a clear sign that more healing is needed.

Soul ties must be broken before stepping into something new. If your sense of peace, joy, and identity is dependent on a man instead of God, you're not yet ready to be found. When you lack self-love and worth, you'll lower your standards and accept less than you deserve. You'll be caught, not found.

- Being caught is temporary.
- Being found is divine and lasting.

Allow God to heal you, even if it takes longer. Protect your investment your heart, mind, emotions, time, and body. Guard your spiritual life and character so that when the right man comes, you're ready. You are on a journey to wholeness, not just for yourself, but for him and your future children. As you grow, you'll recognize that you are an asset, not a liability. This revelation will empower you to move with wisdom and discernment.

When you know your worth, you won't accept less than God's best. This isn't arrogance it's confidence rooted in God's love, not man's approval. For Men

Before you go looking for your "good thing," locate yourself.

Who you are is not what you do. Discovering yourself brings clarity of identity and purpose. Your good thing is divinely connected to that.

How can she be your helpmate if neither of you knows what she's meant to help you with?

Bringing someone into your brokenness is not wise. The moment you feel like you need someone to complete you, it's a sign you're not ready. Allow God to heal your wounds, shift your dependence to Him, and lead you into wholeness.

Men lead best from a place of wholeness, understanding, and spiritual alignment. Men lead even

better when they are led by the Holy
Spirit.

The Holy Spirit teaches you how to
love others but first, you must learn
how to love yourself.

I know men are often not encouraged
to be vulnerable and transparent, but
it's necessary. Ignoring your root
issues will only affect your future
relationships. Invest in your healing
so that when you date, you're not
looking for someone to complete

you but someone to add value to
your life.

Healing is for both men and women.
Self-love is for both men and
women.
Validation and affirmation must
come from God first, or you'll
constantly chase it in people.

It may not be easy. It may take time.
But healing is worth the investment.

Recovery Takeaway:
The Recovery Room is not a place of
shame it's a place of honest healing.
When you let God rebuild you from
the inside out, you won't need
someone to complete you. You'll be
whole, and ready to love from a
place of strength.

Recovery Declaration:
I declare this room is where
resurrection meets reality. The hand
of God is breathing life into what
once was lifeless. My identity,
dreams, confidence, and purpose are

recovering in full measure. I decree that divine alignment is restoring everything stolen, delayed, or buried. This is my comeback season healing isn't just happening in me, it's flowing through me.

Chapter 4 - The Recovery Room Reflection & Journaling

Reflection Moment: What needs to be surrendered in your personal 'recovery room'?

Journal Prompt:

What do you believe God wants to restore in you today?

_____

_____

_____

_____

_____

_____

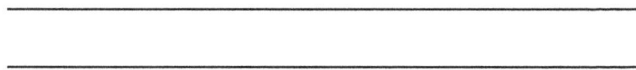

Chapter 5 — Learning to Lead Your Heart

"Above all else, guard your heart, for everything you do flows from it."
— Proverbs 4:23 (NIV)

Guarding What God Gave You

Never allow your heart to lead you learn to lead your heart.

Everyone cannot be trusted with the treasure of who you are. You cannot expect someone to give you love and loyalty if they don't even have it for themselves. When you understand this, you'll stop placing expectations on people that only God can fulfill.

Over time, you'll discover that God is the true source and answer for everything you need. I can recall many moments when I longed for love when I wanted someone to love me deeply and to reciprocate that love. But often, it didn't happen the way I expected. I was left feeling disappointed, discouraged, or hurt.

And each time, I was reminded that only God could provide the comfort and resolution I was searching for. Every time my heart was broken, I could sense Him whispering, "I'm the only one incapable of mishandling your heart."

My focus needed to shift from needing someone to love me to trusting His timing. He would send the one who was worthy of receiving my love when the time was right.

I've never had a problem with that concept, but let's be honest it's not always easy. Yet, God is faithful to walk with you through seasons of transition and change. As you learn to love yourself more, your self-value increases. You become more intentional about protecting your assets and investments your heart, your time, your energy, your gifts, and your purpose.

Protecting Your Investments

Your relationship and intimacy with
God are an investment.
Your relationships with people are
an investment.
Your time, your peace, and your
presence are an investment.

Be intentional about what and who
you invest in. Guarding your heart is
your responsibility no one else's.

If you are pure, you have assets.
If you are educated, you have assets.

If you are spiritual, you have assets. If you have values, morals, and standards, you have assets. If you have wisdom, wealth, or businesses, you have assets. Guard them. Protect them. Keep them. Preserve them.
Because not everyone has your best interest at heart.

Jesus taught us to "love your neighbor as yourself." But if you don't love yourself well, you won't love anyone else well either. The capacity to love deeply comes from

God and grows as you spend time with Him.

This is especially important when it comes to identifying what real love looks like and how it should be demonstrated in your life.
Love in Action

Love isn't just a feeling it's a decision and an action. There are two critical aspects to understand:

1. Loving Yourself

Take the time to get to know yourself.

If you've been hurt, abused, disappointed, rejected, or misunderstood it's okay. We've all been there. But don't rush to connect with someone out of loneliness or desire. Instead, connect with yourself and your Heavenly Father first.

Those experiences must be processed in a healthy environment, in a healthy way. God will help you, and He will send the right people to support you.

Loving yourself means respecting yourself.
It means considering how your actions affect your mind, body, heart, soul, and even your finances.

You do not have to tolerate disrespect or abuse. You have the right and the responsibility to create boundaries that protect your self-awareness and self-worth.

2. Loving Others

Loving others doesn't mean agreeing with everything they say or do. It means respecting them enough to honor their voice, even if their opinion is different from yours.

It means:
- Considering how your words and actions affect them.
- Choosing not to attack when you disagree.
- Seeking to build up rather than tear down.

When you know what love truly is, you'll also know what it isn't. And that clarity will empower you to make better choices when dating or building relationships. You'll recognize red flags, establish boundaries, and avoid unnecessary heartbreak.

The Fruit of Love

"Love is patient, love is kind. It does not envy, it does not boast, it is not proud. It does not dishonor others, it is not self-seeking, it is not easily angered, it keeps no record of wrongs. Love does not delight in evil but rejoices with the truth. It always protects, always trusts, always hopes, always perseveres. Love never fails."

— 1 Corinthians 13:4–8 (KJV) Love will always cause you to:

- Be Patient
- Be Kind
- Reconcile
- Consider Others
- Edify and Encourage
- Value and Respect

- Forgive and Apologize
- Remain Humble
- Put Pride Aside
- See the Best in Others

Recovery Takeaway:
Lead your heart don't let it lead you.
When you love yourself the way
God intended, you protect what
matters, attract what aligns with your
purpose, and love others from a
place of strength rather than
emptiness.

Recovery Declaration:
"I declare that my heart is no longer a slave to emotions, disappointments, or past wounds. I rise in divine strength, leading my heart under the Lord's guidance. Every misplaced affection is being realigned. My expectations are no longer chained to man but anchored in God. From this day forward, my heart will follow divine direction and not temporary emotions. I decree healing, order, and divine timing over every matter of my heart."

Chapter 5 - Learning to Lead Your Heart

Reflection Moment:

Have you been leading your heart— or following your feelings?

Journal Prompt:

What steps can help you start leading your heart with wisdom and grace?

_____

_____

_____

_____

_____

Chapter 6: Know Your Worth

If you're reading this, I'm sure you can look back at certain moments in your life and remember choices you wish you had made differently. If given the chance, you'd probably choose a completely different route. You're not alone this is true for many of us.

But here's the truth: if you remove the journey, you strip away the process that shaped you into who you are today. Growth is rarely comfortable. Not everyone embraces their process or learns from the obstacles they face. But if you're reading this, then somehow even through the pain it has worked for your good. Though the experience may not have been pleasant, the treasure of wisdom, knowledge, and understanding gained along the way is priceless.

This leads to an essential revelation: knowing your worth and understanding what you need in a partner, in relationships, and in life.

Life after divorce taught me a lot especially the power of knowing my worth and value. It teaches you how to carry yourself with dignity, to honor yourself with self-respect, and to never settle for less than what God has called you to receive.

Self-Worth vs. Value

How you see yourself is a reflection of your self-worth.
How others see you is a reflection of your value.

If you want to increase your value, you must first discover your worth.

I've also learned that respect is what you give others; self-respect is what you give yourself. When you respect yourself, it places a demand for others to honor that same standard. You can't make anyone respect you but you can absolutely choose not to remain in spaces where you are not valued. When respect isn't reciprocated, you have the right to make a decision.

You can choose to stay or to walk away. And even in environments like work, where walking away isn't always immediate, you still have the right to speak up about how you're treated. There are laws and policies to protect human dignity for a reason.

On this self-love journey, you'll begin to realize you no longer need to be bound by the opinions of others:

"Will they understand?"

"What will they say?"

When you truly know your worth, you teach people how to treat you. If they're in your life, it's because you gave them permission to be there.

The Power of Meditation

To get to this place of wholeness, you must understand the power of meditation and how it can transform your life from the inside out.

I once heard a quote by Lao Tzu that deeply impacted me:

"Watch your thoughts, they become your words; watch your words, they become your actions; watch your actions, they become your habits; watch your habits, they become your character; watch your character, it becomes your destiny."

Transformation begins in your thoughts. If you choose to think the right thoughts and speak the right words, everything else follows. The hardest part is aligning your thoughts, words, and beliefs but once that alignment happens, everything shifts.

I grew up with a poor self-image because of the negative words spoken over me as a child. Those words shaped how I thought about myself and created a silent, inner dialogue that echoed through my soul. That voice wasn't always external; it was internal, rooted deep within my subconscious.

The Inner Dialogue

There are two voices speaking within our conscious and subconscious. One affirms us; the other tears us down.

• The conscious mind creates, thinks, and decides.
• The subconscious mind responds like autopilot it's programmed by past experiences and beliefs.

When the conscious mind quiets down, the subconscious takes the lead. That's why being aware of your inner dialogue is so powerful. Your thoughts shape your behavior even when you don't realize it.

If we want to master ourselves, we must be aware of what's happening inside of us. If we want to build our self-esteem, we must acknowledge where it's been fractured, trace it back to its root, and allow healing to flow.

That internal conversation you're having determines what you believe about yourself. It shapes how you think, how you speak inwardly, and how you allow others to treat you. Evidence of low self-worth often shows up in how easily we accept mistreatment and confuse it for love.

God's Heart for You

God desires more for you. He loves you deeply but He also wants you to love yourself.
When you change the internal conversation, healing begins. When you know your worth, you stop

begging for what you already
carry.
When you honor yourself, you
position yourself to walk in divine
restoration.

Today, may a new declaration rise
up in you:

"I know who I am. I know what I
carry. I know what I deserve. I am
valuable. I am worthy. I am loved."
When this truth settles in your heart,
restoration and inner healing won't
just visit you they'll dwell in you.

Recovery Takeaway:
Your self-worth is not determined by others but by God's truth about you.
How you see yourself shapes how others will treat you.
Self-respect places a demand for respect in your relationships.

Recovery Declaration:
"I decree and declare that I fully embrace my worth and identity in Christ. Every negative word spoken over me is being uprooted, and the truth of who I am is being established

in my spirit, soul, and body."
"I will no longer see myself through
the lens of rejection, shame, or
comparison. I will see myself as
Heaven sees me; "I am whole, I am
Righteous, and I am Loved by God."

"My voice carries authority. My
presence carries value."
"I declare that my thoughts are aligning
with God's thoughts concerning me.
My inner dialogue is shifting from
defeat to destiny."

"I am no longer at war with myself—
wholeness is my portion. From this day

forward, I walk in divine confidence, self-respect, and unshakable worth. I divorce and detach myself from chaos, and I intentionally and purposely pursue God's peace."

Chapter 6 - Know Your Worth

Reflection & Journaling

Reflection Moment:

Where have you settled for less than you're worth?

Journal Prompt:

How can you honor your value through your daily decisions?

_____

_____

_____

_____

Chapter 7: The Four-Point Process

Investigating and Building Rapport

In this chapter, I want to share a practical relational strategy God gave me a framework that helped me develop stronger communication skills, steward my heart with wisdom, and approach new relationships with emotional maturity. This wasn't just about meeting someone new. This was about guarding my heart while learning how not to mismanage someone else's.

When we're healing, it's easy to let strong feelings move faster than true understanding. You can feel something deeply for someone without having enough information about them and if you're not careful, you end up making long-term decisions based on temporary emotions. That's why emotional regulation is critical. You must separate what you feel from what you know, so that when you speak, it comes from clarity and not confusion.

I learned this lesson the hard way. In 2015, God opened a door for me to work in the car business. I sold cars for about two years, and during that time, I learned how to communicate better skills I didn't have before. I struggled with listening, expressing myself clearly, and engaging with confidence. But through training and daily interaction, those skills grew. I began applying what I learned professionally to my personal life— and it changed everything.

Now, before I go further, let me say this clearly: I can only share what worked for me. You are your own person with your own experiences, background, and beliefs. My hope is not that you duplicate my strategy, but that what I share will inspire new ideas and help you discover your own approach.

Why Investigation Matters

In the car business, there's a structured process we followed to create the ultimate car-buying experience. Skipping steps was possible but never wise. The same is true in dating: no shortcuts.

The first step was Investigating. When a customer walked in, we'd ask targeted questions like:

- "Have you been here before?"

- "Are you working with anyone?"

- "What brings you in today?"

These simple questions revealed why they were there and helped avoid unnecessary conflicts with other consultants. When this step was skipped, problems always showed up later.

I began applying this same principle to my dating life. Too many people jump into relationships without doing the groundwork and then end up paying for it with tears, broken hearts, and soul ties. For years, we've been told to "follow our hearts." That sounds good but if your heart isn't anchored in truth, it can lead you into places your purpose never called you to go.

The heart is regulated by our mind and emotions, which are influenced by our physical senses. So no you can't fully trust your heart when you've just met someone. Many of us haven't developed our spiritual senses enough to discern hidden motives, character flaws, trauma triggers, or nonnegotiable early on. That takes time, and in the meantime, emotions must be checked at the door.

I started asking myself hard questions:

- "Am I leading my heart, or is my heart leading me?"

- "How can I love someone I barely know?"

- "Why am I attaching so quickly without truly discerning?"

- "Why do people give their bodies before they give themselves time to build a solid foundation spiritually, emotionally, and mentally?"

Premature sex can cloud judgment, stir confusion, and create ungodly soul ties. Emotional attachments formed too quickly can blind you to red flags you would have normally recognized. I'm not here to judge anyone's path but if you're serious about healing and building something lasting, don't shortcut the process.

So I ask myself practical, intentional questions early on:

- Do we share core values?

- Are our beliefs in God aligned— or could this cause division later?

- Is there a spiritual connection deeper than physical attraction?

- Are we intellectually and emotionally compatible?

- Do our conversations flow naturally or feel forced?

- Are we aligned on family values, purpose, and future goals?

These questions aren't meant to interrogate the other person they're for me to reflect on. If I'm going to invest my heart, I need clarity, not chaos.

Building Rapport: A Continuous Process

Even when I'm physically attracted to someone, I approach it with respect and self-control. Attraction might catch my attention, but it doesn't dictate my direction. I start by regulating my emotions, keeping conversations appropriate, and listening closely.

As the woman shares, I observe not with judgment, but with awareness. I take mental notes. I reflect on my personal list of preferences, red flags, and non-negotiable that I established during my own healing journey. I've learned to value character over preference. I can adjust my preferences, but I won't compromise my values.

This helps me decide if the connection is worth further investment or if it's simply a friendship. If it feels right to go deeper, then I move on to the next step: building rapport.

Rapport building never ends in healthy relationships. Just like in business, regular "updates" help both people stay in tune with each other as they grow and evolve. When trust is built through open communication, you gain insight not just into the good, but also the parts you'll need to decide whether you can live with long-term.
Here's the reality: when you first meet someone, you only see the best

version of them. It takes time to see how they handle pressure, pain, and real life. That's why this stage is so crucial.

Asking the Right Questions

Rushing into relationships without asking the hard questions creates cracks that often show up later. Some of the questions I've learned to explore over time include:

- Do you have children? Do you want more?

- Have you been married? Would you remarry?

- What did you learn from your last relationship?

- What are your deal breakers and triggers?

- What are your spiritual and religious beliefs?

- How's your relationship with your parents?
- What are your non-negotiable?

These conversations don't all happen at once they unfold naturally. And because I don't shoot my shot prematurely, I'm able to maintain my integrity, guard my assignment, and discern more clearly.

Test Drive and Delivery

Once a salesperson builds trust, they move to the next step: the test drive. No one buys a vehicle without test driving it. In relationships, this "test drive" for me is the dating process the period where both people intentionally do life together before making long-term commitments.

Let's be real: deciding whether to have sex before marriage is a personal conviction between you, your partner, and God. I'm not here to give permission or judge. I'm here to acknowledge reality and emphasize wisdom. People will make their own choices, but choices carry consequences. My responsibility is to steward my heart with the Holy Spirit's guidance.

When both individuals choose to invest fully, the next stage is commitment the engagement process, leading to the altar. My hope and prayer is that when God reveals my "good thing" my confidant, lover, best friend, and life partner I'll stand before her and say "I do" without hesitation.

A Final Word on Value and Standards

Dating today is complex — different backgrounds, different mindsets, endless options. But when you know your worth, you don't settle for confusion. You stop giving discounts on what's priceless.

I've learned from my failures. I've gained wisdom through pain. Now, I walk into new connections with self-awareness, emotional intelligence, and spiritual clarity. I know what I bring, and I trust God to align me with someone who adds value to my life as I do to hers.

May this chapter provoke you to slow down, ask the right questions, build rapport with intention, and let wisdom lead your heart not just your emotions.

Recovery Takeaways:
Emotions should be regulated not allowed to lead decisions. Investigating early in relationships saves years of unnecessary pain.Asking intentional questions protects your heart and clarifies compatibility.

Recovery Declaration:
"I decree and declare that my heart
will be led by wisdom, not impulse.
"I will no longer rush into
relationships without discernment,
prayer, or process." My emotions
will be governed by clarity, not
chaos."

"The Holy Spirit will be my compass
as I discern character, motives, and
alignment."I declare that every
counterfeit connection is being
exposed and removed."

"I attract relationships that are healthy, whole, and God-ordained. "I will build with intentionality, investigate with clarity, and cultivate with purity.

"My future covenant will not be rushed it will be revealed in God's perfect timing.
My heart is protected, my vision is clear, and my love is anchored in truth."

Chapter 7 - The Four-Point Process

Reflection & Journaling

Reflection Moment:

Which part of the Four-Point Process challenged you the most?

Journal Prompt:

How can you begin applying that principle this week?

_____

_____

_____

_____

_____

Chapter 8: Asset vs. Liability

When it comes to relationships, ask yourself honestly:
Am I an asset or a liability?

Before you answer, let's define these terms clearly:

• Asset: Something of value that continues to increase in worth over time. An asset is an investment that strengthens, grows, and does not depreciate.

•   Liability: Something that drains, owes, or diminishes. A liability carries weight without ownership. It can represent emotional, mental, spiritual, or financial debt.

How you answer this question reveals how you see yourself and what you believe you deserve. It's a reflection of your thought life, your self-worth, and your relationship with value.

Self-Perception and Attraction

Sometimes the relationships we attract are mirrors of how we see ourselves. If you constantly attract broken, toxic, or emotionally unavailable people, it may be because there are unhealed places within you that need attention. I've had to ask myself:

"Why do I keep attracting broken people with toxic behaviors?" The answer came in the quiet moments with God. I had to confront the truth:

as long as I allowed others to devalue me verbally, mentally, or emotionally I wasn't stewarding my heart well. I wasn't protecting my own assets.

The turning point came during my marriage. About six and a half years in, I began asking hard questions. After the divorce, I made the decision to step away and heal. In that healing season, I learned something powerful:

"No one can come into my life without my permission, and no one can stay without it either."

If a relationship isn't adding value, it's extracting it. Whether emotionally (due to poor communication), spiritually (because you're unequally yoked), or financially (because one person only consumes) you can end up in arrears. If you're giving and not receiving, and you choose to stay, you're functioning as a liability in your own life.

Healing and Rediscovering Value

Taking intentional time to heal, rediscover your worth, and learn to love yourself is one of the best investments you can make. Once you understand your value, you become more discerning. You'll see red flags earlier. You'll know what your non-negotiable are. And you'll stop wasting time in relationships that drain you.

For me, this journey began when I simply allowed God to love me. His love became my anchor. He affirmed me as a son and friend, but also revealed Himself as Father, Counselor, and Confidant. He was patient when others walked away. He stayed when I felt abandoned. And because of that, I learned I didn't need anyone to complete me. I needed someone who would complement me. Waiting hasn't been easy but I'm confident I will be able to say it worth it.

Biblical Insight: The Cost of Moving Ahead of God

Impatience can be dangerous. We see this in the story of Abraham and Sarah (Genesis 16–18). God promised them a son, Isaac. But when Sarah grew impatient, she took matters into her own hands, asking Abraham to sleep with Hagar. The result was Ishmael — a decision that created years of tension within their home.

Isaac was the son of promise; Ishmael was the son born of the flesh

(Galatians 4:21–31). When we move ahead of God, we often create problems we later have to pray our way out of.

I've learned this lesson personally — it's always better to consult God first before making life-altering relationship decisions.

Recognizing a Liability

When we don't know our value, we tolerate people who drain us:

- People who manipulate, control, or dominate.
- People who constantly withdraw but never deposit.
- People who diminish our mental, spiritual, emotional, or financial strength.

A liability relationship weakens you over time. An asset relationship builds you up.
When you see yourself as an asset, you protect your heart, time, mind, emotions, resources, and spirit like their treasure because they are. This

is what dating with purpose looks like. You know what you want and don't want. You're clear, intentional, and discerning.

Guarding Your Investments

Choosing wisely where and with whom you invest your heart can save you from years of unnecessary pain. Your heart, mind, time, emotions, resources, and spirit are your assets. Protecting them safeguards your purpose and destiny.

If God sends someone into your life, there's purpose attached to it. Covenant marriage isn't random, it's strategic. It reflects God's promise, not just a social contract. It's an alliance built on love, faithfulness, and shared vision. Before you say "I do," choose someone who can weather storms with you, not just enjoy sunny days. Love that endures is rooted in covenant, not convenience.

Learning What Love Is and Isn't

To truly understand love, you must also understand what it is not. That revelation helped me establish healthy boundaries that protect what God has entrusted to me. Wholeness is a lifelong pursuit, but I trust God to complete the work He started in me.

As 3 John 1:2 says:
"Beloved, I wish above all things that you may prosper and be in good health, even as your soul prospers."

Practical Steps Toward Transformation

If this message resonates with your heart, here are a few practical steps to begin your journey:

1. Give your heart fully to Christ. When He isn't your first love, all other relationships risk becoming idolatrous.

"Seek first the Kingdom of God and His righteousness, and all these things will be added to you." — (Matthew 6:33)

2.   Pursue healing intentionally.
Therapy, spiritual counseling,
prayer, and meditation on the Word
of God can all work together to bring
freedom and clarity.

3.   Lay down pride and ego.
Don't self-sabotage your healing by
resisting the process. Surrender the
broken pieces to God and allow Him
to create something beautiful out of
your pain.

Final Reflection:
You are not called to live in deficit.
You are called to live as an asset —
valuable, whole, and purpose-driven.
When you know your worth, you no
longer allow anyone to mishandle
your treasure.

Recovery Takeaways :
Knowing your value determines what
you accept in relationships. Assets
build value; liabilities drain it. If it
doesn't add value, it's extracting it
and you have the power to choose.
Healing and self-love sharpen your
ability to discern red flags early.

God's timing is always better than premature decisions.

Recovery Declaration: "I decree and declare that I am an asset in the Kingdom of God. I will no longer allow people, situations, or fear to devalue what God has placed inside of me."

"I am no longer living in deficit I will walk in overflow. I break agreement with every soul tie, toxic pattern, and mindset that made me believe I had to settle for less."

"My heart, my time, my mind, my emotions, my resources, and my purpose are divine investments, and they will be protected."

"I declare that I will no longer partner with liabilities."God is aligning me with purpose-driven
people who add value, not extract it."

"I will wait for God's promise, not create Ismaels out of impatience." I am whole, I am valuable, and I am chosen."

"My relationships will reflect covenant, not convenience.My future is secure in the hands of the One who called me."

Chapter 8 - Asset vs. Liability
Reflection & Journaling

Reflection Moment:

In what ways have you been an asset to others—or allowed others to treat you like a liability?

Journal Prompt:

What boundaries do you need to set to protect your peace and worth?

_____

_____

_____

_____

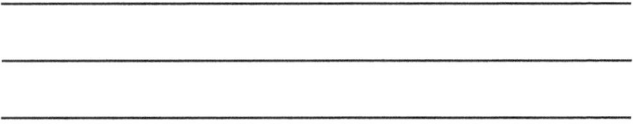

Thank You for Reading

I pray The Recovery Room has inspired healing, self-discovery, and renewed hope in your journey.

If this book has blessed you, please consider leaving a review on Amazon and sharing it with someone who needs encouragement.

Your support helps this message reach others who are still finding their way back to wholeness.

Eric T. Roscoe

Books by Eric T. Roscoe

- The Recovery Room: A Self-Love Journey for the Broken, the Healing, and the Hopeful
- 12 Keys to Kingdom Living
- The Children's Bread: A Journey to Liberation

Connect & Follow

Podcast / YouTube: Building My Life with Eric Roscoe

Instagram: @ericthomasroscoe

About the Author

Eric T. Roscoe is a contemporary Marketplace Prophet, award-winning author, visionary leader, entrepreneur, podcaster, and ambassador for the Kingdom of God. As the founder of Eric Roscoe Global and cofounder and visionary leader of The Salt Hub, a Kingdom resource and training center, Eric is committed to equipping people with tools for spiritual growth, identity, and transformation. In addition to his ministry and leadership work, Eric is a chef in assisted living and memory care, where he serves with excellence and compassion. His multifaceted journey reflects his dedication to purpose, service, and excellence across every sphere of life.

Through his books, teachings, and podcast Building My Life with Eric Roscoe, he inspires others to embrace healing, discover identity, and rise boldly into their Kingdom assignments. Known for his prophetic insight and practical wisdom, Eric blends authenticity with faith to reach people in both spiritual and everyday contexts.Above all, Eric treasures his role as a devoted father to his three daughters Keely, Kylah, and Kalli— who remain his greatest joy and inspiration. His life's mission is to help others heal, build, and live with clarity, courage, and Kingdom purpose.